REGENERATION

ANDREW
ALDRED

ANDREW ALDRED

Published by
Chipmunkapublishing
United Kingdom

http://www.chipmunkapublishing.com

Rocker

You come to see me, and it is not hard to see.
The shelves full of records and crammed with CDs.
The guitars and amplifiers placed around strategically.
I have invested a lifetime in rock and roll and that is me.
It takes all my spare time and all of my money.
You realise this is something I take very seriously.
Signs of a mis-spent youth are everywhere in my house.
If I get a spare moment rock music is what I think about
The neighbours probably wish I would just go away.
But I have spent thirty years learning how to play.
I get a little better and I am taking my time.
If I keep it quiet, I am committing no crime.
My beard and denim jacket gives away who I am.
Just another ageing rocker who does not give a damn.

Vote Left

Donald Trump is finding out he is just one person.
And he cannot make the sweeping changes he wants to
Nigel Farage scares the hell out of me.
Because of the way he wants to change this country
But the constitution will not be overturned easily.
People have rights and they need to make themselves heard.
They will not be able to send all the refugees back.
We need these people here to work for us.
To do the jobs we consider beneath ourselves.
And fill the gaps in the workplace that we will not.
People need to see through the likes of Trump and Farage
Coming on with a lot of idealistic nonsense and bullshit
Labour is a steady government with some good ideas.
That is why they got voted in and we need to keep them.
The local elections are going to be coming up soon.
And Reform are not the people I will be voting for

Something More

I wish there was something more to life.
But I am pushing sixty and there is not.
She has endless TV shows to watch.
And I have a record collection to see to
As well as my guitar, my poetry and my garden
We have lived apart since we got divorced.
It was so traumatic that I could not do it again.
We both have health problems and mental illness.
And sometimes I feel that life is closing in.
It is years since we went on holiday.
And I do not know if we could do it now.
We cook meals and look after our houses.
And I am now a paid carer for my ex-wife.
We struggled for years to try to hold down jobs.
But being who we are we did not have much luck.
We are in a quandary and there is nothing we can do.
We have each other and are chasing life down to nothing.
We have had our chips and there is very little else.

Going Down Fighting

The Ukrainians are very sceptical of Donald Trump
And they do not want to hear what he has to say.
They want Crimea and the territory he has taken.
And sadly, that is not something they can realistically have.
They want things to be how they were before this started.
They are fighting for their homeland and way of life.
As are the Palestinians who live in the Gaza strip?
While the rest of the world has abandoned them
There is no medicine and no aid, and they are starving.
The war is so one-sided it is an annihilation.
The safe areas are gone, and they are attacking hospitals.
We all know it is wrong, but we are powerless.
In that respect it is similar to the war in Ukraine
I am so sorry we cannot do more to help these people.
They are going down fighting and God will take their souls.

Not For Profit

I get paid by the British Army and the DWP
And anything else I am able to do will make no money.
I get a steady wage off these people because I need it.
It enables me to have a life and a standard of living.
I can at least afford musical equipment and records.
That is my interest and what I spend my money on
But as far as being a star or a millionaire forget it.
Disabled people get paid not to cope with that.
They can follow their interests and find something to do.
And they do not have the stress of endless commitments.
They do not have to cope with wealth and public life.
I have never made a penny for my books or my music.
Instead, it has cost me a lot of money to do these things.
The products are good; I get paid and everyone is happy.

Similarities

I sympathise with a lot of you people.
The ethnic minorities who are trying to find a voice
The people who have a different sexuality to most
Anybody who feels isolated or marginalized in any way.
I have a lot of similarities with a lot of people.
But I am not exactly the same and everyone has to fight.
There are millions of different people with different viewpoints.
If you need to be heard, you had better get out there.
And make them listen to you and what you have to say.
We all want a better world and a better way of doing things.
And if you are within the law the rest of us should listen
We are all people struggling through very difficult times.
We are not all the same but there are some broad similarities.

Facebook

I really appreciate everyone who has tried to contact me.
But I am an intensely private person.
My partner Jane takes up all of my time.
And I have always been happy to give my life to her.
I have had countless martial artists try to contact me.
I have had TV presenters and sports stars.
All I can do is congratulate you on who you are.
In another life I would want to know you all
But I am busy with my partner and have very little time.
I am now Jane's carer because she is not well physically.
I take her to appointments and look after her.
We have the love life we are able to have.
And we have always been able to talk to each other.
I know what I am doing with her but cannot have anybody else.
I have what I have got with Jane, and I am happy.
And because I am a paid carer it helps with my bills
All I can say is sorry I have not got back to you.
But know that you have been noted, and you are appreciated.

The Middle Road

The middle road in politics is healthy.
If things go too far left or right beware
Because catastrophe will invariably follow on
You can have labour or conservative for me.
And I will vote for whoever is best at the time.
But when you get to militant socialists or the far right
You are not going to appeal to me in any way.
That is why I am warning you about Nigel Farage
They can talk the hind leg off a donkey in the pub.
And it all sounds very good and plausible to you.
But when you get to the reality of what they are saying
It will divide society and marginalise sectors of it.
That will not be good for the country, and it will take five years.
Before they are voted out and someone else can take over
It has happened in America and created havoc for everyone.
And is America or anyone else really better off?
The answer is no, and we are all left with the same problems.
You do not need to change things that radically.
Because they were more or less right in the first place
The middle ground in politics is where everybody wins.
Change can be divisive and counterproductive for everyone.
And it is not achieved overnight like they would have you believe.

Achieving Nothing

Britain, France and Canada are pissed off with Israel.
And it has taken a hell of a long time to say so.
But we have and the trucks with aid are getting through.
Even though Israel has condemned us for supporting terrorists.
I look at what they are doing and there has got to be a better way.
They want to eradicate Hamas and there is no end.
When can they be happy and let people have their lives?
What do Netanyahu and Israel think they are going to achieve?
When will enough actually be enough for them to stop?
How complete does a victory actually have to be?
Sooner or later all of this will have to be cleaned up.
The people that are left will have to be re-homed.
And if you get rid of every last one of them it is genocide
And whether that is already the case is open to argument
Somehow there has to be a future for those left in Gaza.
Sometime there has to be an end to this war.
And an entire nation that has been reduced to rubble
Has to be replaced and rebuilt with something.
That everybody is satisfied with and has a lasting future

Blind

How did Donald Trump believe that Putin?
Was somebody who would listen to him?
Did he think he was some sort of nice man?
Did he think he could strike a bargain with him?
He should have listened to other world leaders.
He should have put responsibilities above friendship.
Zelensky said Putin would make a fool out of Trump.
And it's alright hating Zelensky for saying so.
But you have to admit he was right all the way.
And America and the rest of us are having to re-think.
About how we deal with the problem of Russia.
Britain and Europe are taking responsibility.
Trump is learning that Putin cannot be trusted.
And maybe he should be supporting Ukraine.
But the war drags on and people are dying.
Trump has to back one side or the other.
That will be the difference in who wins this war.
If you want peace you have to pay for it

Greed and Nonsense

I am appalled at the demands of junior doctors.
They had a huge pay rise last year.
And now they want another huge pay increase.
All it amounts to is greed and stupidity.
People putting themselves above everybody else.
We are not going to get this country on its feet.
If we do not realise, we are all in it together.
And we must all work to make a better future.
That means the junior doctors need to do their bit as well.
They mostly come from privileged backgrounds.
Do they think that everybody should bow down to them?
That they should have what they want when others do not?
Government finances are not a bottomless pit of money.
Everything has to be costed and accounted for
And that includes them and what they do for us.
People should not over-value themselves in this world
Because somebody else will always step in their shoes
And do the job instead of them and do it better.
Because they are grateful for the opportunity and need the money
If you do not want to be a doctor for a doctors pay
Do something else and see whether you are any better off
And do not try to hold the country to ransom for personal gain.

Re-inventing The Wheel

Politicians are so busy cutting corners.
They lose their moral compass completely.
We forget what came out of World War 2
We forget the Geneva convention and social security.
We forget the National Health Service and human rights.
Because we are too busy thinking about money
And we believe people are exploiting out laws.
So, we supposedly change them to our advantage.
But the world seems to have lost its way.
World leaders still want to fight wars.
We somehow have to deal with Netanyahu and Putin
China and America want to grab more territory.
We make a fuss of veterans on VE day.
But we forget what they fought for in the first place.
A lasting peace and laws we would all adhere to
But nobody wants to play by the rules these days.
You cannot re-invent the wheel however hard you try.
It was alright in the first place my friend.
We have all lost sight of the truth that was.
Because all politicians want is to please the public
And everybody wants more money than they can have.

The Lost Generation

The children of today all seem to be ill.
They all seem to be on the autistic spectrum.
They do not want to work in society.
All they want to do is play video games.
These might seem to be sweeping statements to you.
But there is a genuine problem with our youth.
One in eight people in their twenties is out of work.
How are we going to support an aging population?
The sad fact is that we are not going to be able to
The youth of today are going to have to get up.
And do something for society and the rest of us.
Or society will implode and there will be anarchy.
The lost generation had better catch on quickly.
Because the free rides will be over pretty soon
If you are capable of working for a living
That is exactly what you should be doing.
Do not ask me to support you to do nothing.
I have done my bit for a lot of people.
It's your world and its down to you.

Volatile

People like Donald Trump and Elon Musk are volatile.
If they do not get exactly what they want they raise hell
And there are a lot of people like this in power at the moment.
People who struggle to tolerate each other never mind the rest of
us.
Reform have had a falling out with their party chairman.
If you do not consider other people you will end up alienating
them
If you want to be openly racist you will upset a lot of people
People with volatile political views are extremely divisive.
And even if they win elections they fall out amongst themselves.
You will always need someone steady and reliable in charge.
Somebody who gets the job done and does not upset anybody else.
This is why Nigel Farage and Donald Trump are not fit for office.
Volatile people end up causing trouble because they do not listen.
Putin and Netanyahu are examples of people who are socially
inadequate.
And a lot of people at the top need replacing these days.

Right Wing Thugs

There has been a series of race riots recently.
First in Southport after the murder of three girls
Now in Ireland after the suspected rape of a girl
There is an emergence of civil unrest because of thugs.
Who go after refugees and people of foreign origin?
They believe they are right to do so but who is behind them?
Who is it that is orchestrating all of this violence?
It will probably be some of the illegal far right people.
They need to be stopped and put in jail where they belong.
Because most people come here to work and do a good job
The thugs that go after them do not contribute anything.
All they can do is tear down the community they live in
They are the real cancer in society and should be dealt with
Newsreaders try to make excuses for them because they are white.
They try to understand the point these people are making.
But they overlook the fact that they are breaking the law.
And the only way they can be educated is by going to prison.
All of these people ought to be off the streets and working.
And they should want to go home and stay there at the end of the day.
There are far too many young people who have lost their way.
No role models, no education, no future or employment
And some bunch of people pulling strings to organise riots for them.
It is all so wrong and an increasing problem that has to be dealt with

Exploited

I did not get a letter to say I was discharged.
Or a phone call or any other form of communication
The last time I saw the psychiatrist he took the piss.
So, I saw the appointment through and walked out.
These people pretend they are your only friend.
While they are busy pulling you apart behind your back
It would not surprise me if social services were to blame.
For my forty years of illness and inability to achieve
What should have been mine and was blighted by mental illness?
All the psychiatrist did was perpetuate my misfortune.
There was no treatment, only an illness that got worse.
They are largely to blame for the crime I committed.
They left me without care and would not see me.
The medication they give you helps you survive.
And it also perpetuates your illness until it burns out.
There is no pot of gold at the end of the rainbow for me.
I am who I am, and I have got what I have got.
Mental health services pull the wool over your eyes.
And use you for their purpose and not yours
I have always rejected my illness and their jurisdiction.
They can have their illness back because they are sick.
They gave me an illness I did not want and wasted my time.
It has taken me forty years to be free of these people.

Sex Crimes

There has been a review into child abuse recently.
The far right want to blame it all on Asian men.
But let me tell you it is far more widespread than that.
There will never be enough space in prison for those involved.
If you want a workforce, you cannot lock them all up.
Those who have been raped, particularly children, deserve help.
And let's not forget it does not only happen to girls.
There are plenty of boys and young men who are also victims.
This is a problem that will never be eradicated from society.
It has always gone on and it always will.
Keir Starmer will do very well not to tackle this head on
The people who are dealing with it are forever fudging issues.
Because they know those involved and there are too many
complicit people
The conservatives let it slide and did nothing.
The far-right entirely misjudge the problem and have no solution.
Starmer will have to provide some sort of token of something
being done.
But too many adults abuse their own children and other people's.
Mentally ill people are taken advantage of by society.
They have no voice and nobody to stand up for them.
There seems to be a need to have this problem in society.
There are too many abusive people who do not know how to
behave.
And unfortunately, most of these people seem to end up in charge.

Israelis At War

Not content with obliterating Gaza they are going after Iran.
They want to wipe out all of their enemies at once.
But will they ever live safely and in peace again?
I really do not know how all of this will pan out.
Their politicians think they are doing the world a favour.
They are saying we will thank them later for what they are doing.
But America is not jumping in on their side anymore.
If they want to fight Iran, they must do it alone.
Iran and Israel definitely want to have a go at each other.
Oil prices will go up and the rest of the world will suffer.
There always has to be a better way than this.
They should have used the Americans to mediate.
They should have listened to others before going it alone.
It's alright hating people but are you ever going to be friends?
What on earth is going to happen when all of this is over?
Could Iran have nuclear arms and be responsible?
God knows others do and we had all better hold back.
If I were an Israeli or an Iranian, I would choose peace and
prosperity.
And I would avoid an all-out war at any cost.

Not Our War

The Americans have refused to help us with Ukraine.
And maybe we should refuse to help them with Iran.
I know we will probably be straight in there.
But to be honest with you this is not our war.
The Iranians and the Americans have long been at loggerheads.
The Iranians and the Jews have long been enemies.
The Iranians sell us oil, and we are happy to buy it.
And I really wish we could all get along better than we do.
Russia and China are standing in the background to all of this.
America needs to be careful and so do its allies.
Because we do not want a worse situation on our hands
This country is just beginning to get back on its feet.
Increased oil prices will be quite enough to cope with
Without buildings being blown up and people hacked to death
I know Iran in some ways is not a friendly state.
And Israel and America want to deal with the problem now.
But I think we should stand back and let them do it.

You Cannot Have It Both Ways

There is an Irish rap band called kneecap.
Who have been inciting antisemitic violence?
And there is also an artist called Bob Vylan
Who has been calling for the death of Israeli troops?
Does this protest have any place in Glastonbury?
The answer is a resounding "No!"
Like the Free Palestine people, they think they can do anything.
And people will just suffer them and their point of view.
You cannot destroy buildings and military assets.
And somehow think you are right in doing so.
I agree Israel has gone beyond too far in Gaza.
But there are peaceful ways of protesting and having your view
heard.
You cannot have a riot at a trial and be within the law.
And these people need to be taught a valuable lesson.
You are either a criminal or a law-abiding citizen, not both.
You cannot have your cake and eat it again and again.
Glastonbury should be all about the music and nothing else.

At Least They Listen

The government has done some U turns recently.
About winter fuel and personal independence payment
People moan about the fact that they have changed their mind.
At least they listen to the public and their views.
At least they take the time to hopefully get things right.
We have had Margaret Thatcher and the poll tax in this country.
And Donald Trump is doing what the hell he wants in America.
People do nothing but moan about the government.
They are already thinking of voting for Reform after Labour
But the truth is the voting public are very fickle people.
They put the government down even if it is doing well.
We should all be grateful we do not live in a war zone.
Because sometimes I think that is what the voting public want

Popularist Politics

It is a very hard thing to keep everybody pleased all of the time.
There is simply never enough money to be able to do that.
Because of the rise in autistic people others will lose out
And a lot of disabled people are going to have to do without their benefits.
I know my case will be up for review soon and I might not get anything.
Because of the new rules designed to make it more difficult to get benefits
Disabled people do not make a lot of money for the country, but they do spend it.
The money they get from the government all goes back into the economy.
But the welfare bill is too high, and a lot of people will have to tighten their belts.
They cannot raise taxes because working people contribute to the economy.
And should not be penalised anymore than they are for doing so.
You cannot please all the people all of the time and this is evident.
Difficult decisions are made, people are prioritised and some lose out.

Chic

The highlight at Glastonbury this year was Chic.
The singers in Nile Rodgers band could really deliver.
Bernard and Nile on bass and guitar were outstanding.
The drummer also sang and had the crowd on its feet.
The keyboard player was outstanding and could also sing.
You get a band like this, and they make the others look cheap.
Because they are so good at what they do, and they have the songs.
Gary Numan and Pulp had their slot and were successful.
With Neil Young unfortunately nobody really took an interest
Rod Stewart looked great but struggled with his voice.
Bob Vylan and Kneecap have probably ruined their careers.
There were new artists like Olivia Rodrigo, Jade and Charli XCX
But Chic stole the show for me and were well worth seeing.

Benefits Britain

When is everyone going to realise?
That they cannot live off the government.
That mum and dad will not bail them out forever.
That autism alone does not mean you cannot work.
That you can only be on one side of the law.
I look at the people around me.
And realise how little we do for the economy.
God knows I have tried everything.
I have made a living out of an illness.
Where I have been raped at night
Because I have been unfit to do anything else
I have slogged my guts out in a warehouse.
I have taught other people how to write.
I have taught them how to use computers.
I served in the army until I got a pension.
And I have done voluntary work for nothing.
I am fifty-nine years old, and I am exhausted.
But I still make the effort to care for my ex-wife.
I do not know how it is for everyone else.
But this government is serious about work.
And the fact that many people do not want to
Reform is going to spend more money on benefits.
How the fuck is that going to work for the economy?
Just have twenty kids and you will be alright.
The state will pay for you not to work.
I am sick of the way we are carrying on.
But my time for making a difference has been and gone.
It really is time to tighten up the benefits system.
Benefits Britain is no good for anyone or anything.

Our Worst Enemy

The worst enemy we have in this world is ourselves.
Everybody seems to want to take advantage.
Whether its doctors and binmen wanting more money
Kids wanting to draw benefits all their working lives.
Politicians wanting to use power for their own ends.
Women wanting to disfigure themselves to look better.
People complaining about global warming but doing nothing.
The list just goes on and on without an end.
We are not on the same side, and everyone wants to be heard.
But we all talk so much self-centred bullshit.
Most of the people on television are no use at all.
And we are supposed to aspire to them for guidance.
We are all wandering about like a bunch of lost children.
I think I will make a cup of tea and forget about today.

What a Mess

The Americans are getting excited about Patriot missiles.
Apparently, some European countries want to buy them.
And give them to Ukraine to fight off the Russians.
Apparently, Trump has agreed to this after talking to his wife.
Donald Trump does not think the Epstein files are important.
And all this after messing around with everybody's tariffs.
A lot of important issues seem to be being fudged at the moment.
And I will be amazed if anything gets done about any of them.
Trump has given Putin fifty days to come to an agreement.
But like Netanyahu and everyone else he is not listening
There is no co-ordination between nations anymore.
People are carrying on regardless and doing what they want.
We all seem to be wading ever deeper in a sea of mud.
And unless the people at the top can actually show some leadership
And get something done this is how it is going to be.

Unsustainable

Everything is supposed to be at breaking point.
From the state of the rivers and the water companies
To the pay of doctors and binmen on strike
Everyone wants the wars in Israel and Ukraine to be over.
But the people at the top and the rest of us cannot agree.
The prison system and the courts are at breaking point.
We need more reservoirs because there is not enough water.
And unsustainable just seems to be the new normal.
Everything is broken in this godforsaken world.
But it keeps turning and we all just carry on.
Todays unsustainable will become tomorrow's disasters.

Walking Away

I am walking away from the mental health service.
I am walking away from the neighbourhood and the community.
My mother is buried, and my father will not last much longer.
I will at last be able to rest in my own bed at night.
The rest of the world has held me back for sixty years.
But I will be free to do what I want to do.
With no judgement or jurisdiction from the world at large
I am keeping my girlfriend, my house and my possessions.
They are things I have suffered for and will not let go of
But a lot of this world is nothing more than a memory to me.
I am withdrawing from this life while I am still able to

Lawsuits

There are a lot of people who refuse to believe the truth.
Even when it is thoroughly proven and is about them.
Take Donald Trump and his birthday card to Jeffrey Epstein
John Torode and his outburst of racist language
You cannot always prove wrong is right in court.
And it would be dangerous and counterproductive to try to
Lawsuits are for people who have got money to waste.
Coleen Rooney and Rebecca Vardy come quickly to mind.
I am sure we would love to know the truth, but do we care?
You can pay a lawyer millions to make the truth disappear.

Be Who You Are

If people were happy with who they are and what they have got
The world would certainly have a lot less problems.
If Vladimir Putin did not want Europe to be part of Russia
If Israel and Hamas did not want each other's territories.
You know you cannot screw the nation and keep what you have at home.
You might wonder why you ever bothered when you see the results.
You cannot live in an Omaze house and not pay the energy bills.
So why did you not carry on living in a terraced house in the first place?
You can change the shape of your body, but you will still have to live in it.
You can be someone else until you have spent all your money.
What was wrong with you in the first place? Dummy!
If we could all be happy with who we are and what we have
Life probably would not get much worse for us or anyone else.

Appalling Organisation

Who would want to be a Christian nowadays?
After the terrible press the church has received
All of the paedophiles hiding in its organisation.
The conversion ceremonies to get rid of homosexual devils.
This society owns more land in the UK than anyone else.
And King Charles the head of state is in charge of it.
I do not believe in the same God as the church does.
They hate homosexuals but that is what most of them are.
Then there are the graveyards for the children born out of wedlock
There are endless stories of abuse that stem from the church.
They say they will clean it up, but I think they should forget it.
Why do we need a God when this is how he is represented?
Religion should be something good, but people make it repulsive.

Powerless

We watch them starving on television every day.
Everyone is blaming each other for the tragedy.
We talk tough but we do not want to upset Israel.
They are supposedly our allies, and we just stand back.
We are letting the Palestinians die and we are powerless.
And all that goes through your head is it could be you.
Life is hard enough for most people without war.
Without climate change, poverty starvation and drought
As well as the horrific injuries we see on television.
I watch this every day, and it makes me ashamed to be human.

Greed

The resident doctors still want more money.
After the highest pay rise anyone got last year
They have been getting overtime for the backlog.
They care more about money than they do about us.
A junior doctor might not get a king's ransom.
But they get twice as much money as I do.
And believe me I am grateful for what I get.
A soldier's pension, PIP and carers allowance
And that is a lot for someone who no longer works.
Do they really want to be doctors at all?
Do they want to privatise the NHS?
Or should they all just be honest thieves?
There is only so much money and we all have to live.

Refuge in Rock n Roll

My dad is dying, and my mother has passed away.
My brother is the only member of my family left.
My girlfriend has also lost her mother who was her friend.
Her daughter and grandson do not come to visit very often.
We are both mentally ill and have persistent physical problems.
She likes the television, and I take refuge in rock n roll.
I listen to my records and play my guitar, and I am somewhere
else.
It takes me away from my life while I am occupied with it.
We rarely go out and I visit her every day.
We are prisoners in our houses and content to be so.
The outside world is a hostile place and people do not understand.
They do not know me and think I can do whatever I want.
I do not have the energy to work never mind be a rock star.
They wonder why I do not talk and do not want to know.
At least Jane has her television, and I have rock n roll.

Futile

I watched them fighting over the food on television.
That had been dropped from an aeroplane.
They are just as bad as everyone else in this.
They are not sharing it out just grabbing what they can.
The ones with knives and sticks get the biggest share.
You are risking getting shot just going to the scene.
And I have to laugh because it does not get any worse
When will people call a halt to all of this madness?
When will the population stop behaving like hungry animals?
Why do we treat each other in such an appalling manner?
From the initial assault by Hamas to the obliteration of Gaza
The starvation and resultant violence over food
What the hell do you do with a situation where it is all so wrong?
Are people fighting and killing each other because they want to?
Will people look back one day and realise how futile it all was?

Religious Maniacs

You know if we all carried on living as Muslims.
We may as well be in Pakistan or Saudi Arabia
But we are not. Thank God we are in the United Kingdom
And we do not have to live as Muslim fundamentalists under
Sharia law.
The women do not have to cover their faces and bodies.
And we can all carry on how we want as long as we are not
breaking state laws.
We have become a lot less prejudiced about a lot of things.
Homosexuality is accepted and rock n roll is not the devil's music.
We do not have to be in the dark ages fighting the crusades
anymore.
Hopefully we can all be accepted and get on with living our lives.
But there are some religious maniacs who would not have this.
They turn to terrorism and to sexually abusing people.
These people are possessed by the devils they are trying to fight.
It is the same in Christianity and other religions as well.
People trying to strike back because of the things they do not
understand.
They think we should all live by a book that is thousands of years
old.
And not only that we should do it to the bloody letter.
People obsessed with religion are a lot of the devil in this world.
They need to get on with their lives and leave others alone.

Emancipation

A lot of people have had their hooks in me.
And I have painstakingly pulled them out one by one.
I suffered at school and through my early life.
Set upon by teachers and pupils I was a lonely boy.
Then I went through the army with its discipline and brutality
I came out of it and set about getting an education.
I went through the prison system and mental health services.
I was on a section without time limit but that is now at an end.
I worked until I could not cope with working any longer.
I tried to look after the relatives that stood by me.
I have been married and although divorced am with the same girl.
But now I have some time to myself and a place of my own.
I have a partner for life and am not looking for anyone else.
I live in a community that sees fit to leave me to my own devices.
And I do try to let people get on without any hindrance.
I have my freedom, and this is the better world I was hoping for.
I no longer owe anyone anything and this is my emancipation.
I have a lot less to give and whatever I had has been taken.

Regeneration

Bolton and Farnworth have been under regeneration recently.
Several large sites have been built and are completed.
There are more houses available for everyone to live in
There are also a lot of immigrants and less white British people.
And there are those amongst us who do not agree with this.
But I am happy to see the redevelopment and the infrastructure.
And I do not care who is living there or next door.
Hopefully the area can move from being run down to prosperous.
And those that do not like it will change their opinions.
We should embrace the change because it will not change back.
New buildings and a new population are here to stay now.

Problems With Parcels

My parcel got stuck south of Manchester.
It was on its way from Tamworth to Bolton
It went off the radar and re-emerged in Manchester.
Two days later it is out for delivery.
But they came when I was out and absent.
All this time I have been communicating by email.
Watching the tracking on the courier's website
But today it is being redelivered, and I will be in
And hopefully I will have no more parcel problems.

The Nuclear Deterrent

I saw them commemorate Hiroshima and Nagasaki
It was eighty years since the nuclear bombs.
They talk of peace and a world without nuclear weapons.
But I would remind everybody that it stopped the war.
And the threat of it is so terrible it has not happened since.
We will never forget the suffering and hardship.
And the great price Japan paid to the allies.
Nuclear bombs are a great deterrent and a terrible threat.

Will They Listen?

The war in Ukraine and Gaza rumbles on
People are dying in droves every day.
Donald Trump wants to put it right.
He would like to see peace in Gaza.
He keeps warning Israel not to go too far.
He is friends with Russia's president Putin.
But he also sympathises with Ukrainian casualties.
President Zelensky does not want to submit territory.
But it is already taken, and he must be realistic.
Could Trump be the man to put all of this right?
He is a maverick and an unconventional president.
But he is the voice of reason in these conflicts.
Will they listen to him or go their own way?

Real Life Stories

There are some terrible real-life stories on TV.
I tend to avoid watching them. I get too involved.
I do not need a television show to play with my emotions.
I find my day-to-day life hard enough any way.
If I can drive my car without being a nervous wreck
If I can deal with my relationship without losing my temper
If I can be kind to all of the people, I am dealing with.
It will take all my energy, and I will be doing well.
It is a long time since I saw anything enlightening on TV.
Or anything that really moved me I could get into
It is all formula this and that and you like it, or you don't.
Real life stories remind me far too much of myself and my
problems.

Hope for a Better World

There is always hope that life will be better.
If you have faith that things will be better than they were
The more of you there are the more it will be achieved.
Do not waste your time seeking out misery and violence.
There is plenty of it around and sometimes you cannot avoid it.
All there is on TV is sex, violence, vice and murder.
And if that is all you have time for look for something better
We do not always have to live in a state of war.
Poverty and disease do not always have to be prevalent.
But you have to experience the bad to appreciate the good
Always know yourself and what it right for you
You will find your way and things will turn around.
If you believe things will be alright, they almost always are.

Hope You Find Love

Existence can be very hard.
In a world where nobody loves you
When people have had enough
And everybody turns their backs.
But whoever you are.
And whatever you have done.
There is always some redemption.
You may not find it in human form.
A pet may be the best friend you have.
Maybe you will never have children.
Or bring someone else's up.
Try to be nice to people.
Try to do what is right.
And I hope you find somebody.
To warm your lonely nights

Never Give Up

Sometimes I am in denial.
Sometimes things get too much.
But I can honestly say.
I never gave up on your love.

Love is not for the weak
We have got to be strong.
Life will pull us apart.
We must always hold on.

At the end of the end
There is always something new.
Hardly ever a dull moment
Always something to do.